1-98

THE
GREAT ANTLER AUCTION

by SUSAN E. GOODMAN   photographs by MICHAEL J. DOOLITTLE

ATHENEUM BOOKS FOR YOUNG READERS

TO SYLVIA AND IRVING GOODMAN—
BETWEEN ONE'S LOVE OF WORDS
AND THE OTHER'S LOVE OF NATURE,
I WAS HALFWAY THERE
—S.E.G.

TO GRETCHEN AND JERRY,
WHOSE SONS WERE ALMOST SCOUTS
—M.J.D.

ACKNOWLEDGMENTS:

We would like to thank the Scouts and their leaders who invited us along, especially the Lindeburgs, who went far out of their way. Thanks to Jim Griffin, Mike Hedrick, and Bruce Smith at the National Elk Refuge for their ready information and technical review, Elkhorn Designs, and Bill Helprin and Grand Plains Wildlife Institute. Shelley Simonton of Jackson's Chamber of Commerce lined up the generous support of Sue and Mark Nowlin of Nowlin Creek Inn, Jackie Williams of R. C. Richards B&B, Eagle Rent-A-Car, Jackson Hole Car Rental, and Continental Airlines.

Thanks to readers Deborah Hirschland and Marjorie Waters for their comments, Anne Scatto for her design, and Marian Armstrong for answering every question that came her way.

A special thanks to George Nicholson for all his kind help. And to Marcia Marshall, who was, as always, indispensable.

Historical photos courtesy of Teton County Historical Society

ATHENEUM BOOKS FOR YOUNG READERS
An imprint of Simon & Schuster Children's Publishing Division
1230 Avenue of the Americas
New York, New York 10020

Text copyright © 1996 by Susan E. Goodman
Photographs © 1996 by Michael J. Doolittle

Designed by Anne Scatto/PIXEL PRESS

The text of this book is set in Monotype Columbus.

First Edition

Printed in Hong Kong

10 9 8 7 6 5 4 3 2 1

Library of Congress Cataloging-in-Publication Data
Goodman, Susan E.
The great antler auction / by Susan E. Goodman; photographs by Michael J. Doolittle.
p. cm.
Includes bibliographical references.
Summary: A Boy Scout program in Jackson, Wyoming, collects elk antlers and sells them at auction to help pay for an elk feeding program at the National Elk Refuge.
ISBN 0-689-80131-9
1. Elk—Wyoming—National Elk Refuge—Juvenile literature. 2. Antlers—Juvenile literature. 3. Boy Scouts—Wyoming—Jackson Region—Juvenile literature. 4. Wildlife conservation—Wyoming—National Elk Refuge—Juvenile literature. 5. National Elk Refuge (Wyo.)—Juvenile literature. [1. Elk. 2. Antlers. 3. Boy Scouts—Wyoming. 4. Wildlife conservation. 5. National Elk Refuge (Wyo.) 6. Boy Scouts of America—Wyoming.] I. Doolittle, Michael J., ill. II. Title.
QL737.U55G66 1996
599.73'57—dc20 95-33381

CONTENTS

SCOUTING FOR TREASURE

"Blue skies, warm weather, what a great day for our Antler Pick Up," said Jim Griffin, assistant manager of the National Elk Refuge in Jackson, Wyoming. He and hundreds of Boy Scouts, Cub Scouts, Scout leaders, and parents were going out onto the Refuge to collect the antlers male elk had shed that spring.

n one month's time, these antlers would be sold at an auction in Jackson's town square. Some of the money would go to the Boy Scouts. But most would help the animals who supplied the antlers in the first place. Eighty percent of the profits would combine with government money to feed hungry elk who spent their long, cold winters on Jackson's Elk Refuge.

"When you get out there," continued Jim, "you might still find some elk left on the Refuge. You don't have to worry about them because they are going to worry about you. Elk will move wherever you aren't. In fact, you'll be helping us. We're trying to encourage them to leave for their summer feeding grounds up north.

Jim Griffin was right about elk being afraid of people. Although elk on the Refuge are used to the feed trucks, they will stampede in reaction to trespassing walkers and skiers.

"Whatever you do," he warned, "stay away from the bison. If you meet up with one unexpectedly, get out of there. You really don't want to tangle with a bison.

"We have already picked up a few thousand pounds of antler and stored it away," Jim said, finishing up his announcement. "Let's see how much we can add to it today."

Although the annual Antler Pick Up is usually set for the third Saturday in April, male or bull elk drop their antlers according to their own schedule. Most bulls lose their antlers in March and April. Rangers gather many of the "early drops," especially if they can be seen from the road. The rangers aren't trying to spoil the Scouts' fun. Antlers are so valuable they must be saved from poachers who sneak onto the Refuge to grab them.

But now it was the Scouts' turn. The Refuge had been divided into eight huge zones. Each Boy Scout troop and Cub Scout pack had an assigned area to comb for treasure.

The boys were told to stay in sight of their leaders but, on this part of the Refuge, that's easier said than done.

Parades of cars, vans, and trucks set off in all directions. Bumping their way to the brown rolling hills of zone one, the Scouts in Troop 200 and Pack 268 talked about the different ways to hunt for antlers.

"I just keep my eyes open for something almond colored," said Adam. "And I look real hard. Even if you just see one tip, it could turn out to be a huge antler with seven points."

Other Scouts based their strategies upon what elk do to shed their antlers. Antlers loosen up and start itching when they're getting ready to drop. To help them along, elk push the antlers against trees. They catch the tips in bushes or muddy stream bottoms and twist to help them break free.

Although the Scouts were the only humans allowed to collect antlers on the Refuge, they had some competition. Animals like porcupines and squirrels nibble on antlers to add minerals and calcium to their diet.

6

So the Scouts knew that stream beds were good places to look. They also planned to search in bushes and around trees. Scouts who had been on many hunts knew to look in ditches. Sometimes antlers were so wobbly, they knocked loose when bulls jumped down into a ditch.

The second their cars and vans stopped rolling, the Scouts were on the hunt. First-timers were surprised at how tough it was to spot the antlers. Seeing a light brown antler hidden in light brown sagebrush wasn't quite as hard as finding a needle in a haystack. But it was a whole lot harder than finding a bottle of ketchup in the refrigerator.

Somebody asked Billy Griffin, a Scout on his sixth hunt, if finding antlers gets any easier with experience. "A little, because you know where to look," he answered, "but mostly you get taller so it's easier to see."

Success at last. "It's antler heaven!" one Scout shouted as he spotted first one antler, then another buried in a nest of fallen logs.

As the day wore on, the kids dragged their finds along with them. One antler, two antlers, no problem.

Sometimes spotting an antler was a lot easier than retrieving it.

Four or five antlers were pretty hard to carry. Some Scouts brought rope to tie their antlers into bundles. Others made do using jackets or even their shirts.

As one Scout walked along, he remembered the elk carcass he saw on last year's hunt. Just as he got close enough to see if the carcass had antlers, the "dead" bull scrambled up and bounded away. Elk are large members of the deer family, second in size only to moose. The Scout said with a grin, "I guess you could say I was a little scared."

Elk backbones made good machine guns.

"Last year we found about fifty antlers," said his friend who was getting tired of running up to patches of sagebrush, only to find sagebrush. "This year all I've seen are rocks, jawbones, and a lot of . . ." he struggled with the best way to express his thought, ". . . a lot of elk crap."

"Don't exaggerate," said the first Scout. "We've also found a lot of bison crap."

Meanwhile, over the ridge, some Cub Scouts found a pair of antlers that had been sawed off their owner. During the past winter, poachers had snuck onto the Refuge to kill this bull—for meat, not for antlers. These illegal hunters clearly decided it was easier to drag off the six- or seven-hundred-pound body without another twenty pounds of antler.

The boys were outraged. "I wish I could catch them and put them in jail," said Jason.

"This antler looks like a dagger," said one Scout. "I'm ready for combat."

"Whoa, it just stabbed me," this Scout said, carrying his six-pointer.

On their treasure hunt, the Scouts also found old bottles, a horseshoe, and this note that drifted to the Refuge in a balloon.

"Hey," said his friend, "maybe we could fingerprint the antlers and find out who it was."

The boys might not have been able to catch the poachers, but by the end of the day, the Scouts had snagged a mountain of antlers. Each of them had walked miles in their search. Some trudged back looking like human coat racks, antlers hung all over their bodies.

"You know, last year, I felt sort of bad because we did all this work and the Refuge got all the money," one Scout said as he rode back in a pickup truck piled high with antlers. "But then I thought it's really the elk that get the money. That's a lot better."

Antlers were not all they found. "That bison must have eaten a lot of grass," this Scout said. "Woof!"

Springtime's increasing daylight acts as a signal for bull elk to shed their antlers. New antlers start growing right away from the bumps called pedicles on top of the elk's skull. Antlers grow very fast, up to an inch a day.

ALL ABOUT ANTLERS

They may seem alike, but horns and antlers aren't the same. The horns on animals like cattle, buffalo, and sheep grow slowly over a lifetime and don't fall off. Antlers, on moose, elk, and deer, are usually larger and branch in different directions. Antlers drop off each winter or spring, so growing them is a yearly job.

It's a lot of work to grow big and heavy antlers that end up falling off. Why bother? To grow these antlers, bulls must be big and healthy themselves. Huge antlers become their advertisement to all the elk around. To the females, these antlers are like a neon sign that says, "Come check me out. I've got good genes to pass on."

To the other males, the antlers say, "I'm in good shape. Better not mess with me." Sometimes just the sight of those huge antlers will make smaller males turn away. Bigger bulls with larger antlers

While they grow, the sensitive antlers are nourished and protected by a furry layer of skin called the velvet. In August, when antlers are full-grown, the velvet dries and sheds off. Elk help it along by rubbing their now hard, white antlers against trees. Juices from trees and shrubs stain the antlers brown.

Older bulls have from five to seven, and occasionally even more points on each antler. The number of points on an older elk's antlers depend upon his age, health, and diet. He needs to be healthy to carry a set of antlers weighing up to twenty-five pounds.

Yearling bulls (between one and two years old) have spikes, which are antlers without branches. The next year, their antlers will probably have three to four branches on each side.

usually win in a fight, and get the chance to pass their genes on to the next generation by mating with the females. This system ensures that future generations are strong and healthy because they have strong, healthy parents.

But after breeding season, a pair of heavy antlers is no longer an advantage. The answer nature has come up with? Dump them and grow new antlers when they are needed.

Before fighting, one bull tries to scare off another by rushing at his opponent and hitting the ground with his antlers. If neither bull gives in, they lock antlers, then push and twist. Occasionally both bulls die when they can't unhook their antlers.

Cows, who don't have antlers, fight by getting up on their hind legs and boxing.

11

The Moulton Homestead today

chapter 2

THE ELK REFUGE

To get to the Refuge for Pick Up Day, the Scouts came from their homes
all over the valley. Their houses, the roads they traveled on,
Jackson's restaurants, stores, and movie theaters are all built
on what used to be the elk's winter grazing land.

ABOVE: The Crail
family ran the post
office in 1910.

BELOW: Homesteaders
and ranchers
moved into the
valley that was the
elk's winter home.

The elk spend summers in the meadows and canyons of the Teton Mountains, of Bridger-Teton National Forest, and in the southern part of Yellowstone National Park. But by fall, cold winds sweep the high country and storms blanket it with very deep snow. Then the elk, or *wapiti* as the Shawnee Indians call them, drift down the mountains in search of food. They come into the valley where they are still able to paw through the snow to get at the grass underneath.

For centuries, a herd of about 25,000 elk migrated from mountains to valley in winter and back to the mountains each spring. Then, just over a hundred years ago, white settlers began to make the valley *their* home. Elk found their journey blocked by fences and homesteads. The grasses they used to eat were harvested into haystacks for farmers' cattle.

Even before the pioneers, some elk would starve during very hard winters. But in years like 1909, 1910, and

Ranchers fed the starving elk all they could spare, but it was not enough to save them.

1911, winters were so cold, snows so deep, the valley so filled with farmers and ranchers, that disaster struck. Elk began to starve in horrifying numbers. They became so hungry they lost their fear of people. Some tried to jump through barn windows to eat with the cattle. One even walked up to a cabin and ate the bristles off a new broom.

Some farmers tried to help, spreading out haystacks for the hungry elk. Still, a few haystacks weren't enough when thousands of elk needed pounds of grass each day to live. Nearly three-quarters of the elk calves never made it through their first winter. So many elk died that one settler said he could walk for a mile on elk bodies without ever stepping off.

When some of the Scouts discussed this tragic era in the elk's history, Troy said, "It was just so horrible and sad. You wouldn't want to go anywhere outside."

Josh agreed. "I wouldn't be able to handle seeing that—all those dead animals and feeling like I couldn't help.

The state of Wyoming began a program to feed the elk in winter.

14

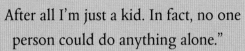

After all I'm just a kid. In fact, no one person could do anything alone."

After those terrible winters, the people of Jackson turned to the government for help. In 1912, Congress gave money to buy 2,760 acres of land for the National Elk Refuge. Today, the Refuge is nearly 25,000 acres. But its miles of hills and plains are still only one-quarter of the land the elk used to have as their winter home. The Refuge is still too small to supply enough grass for 7,500 elk each November through April. That's why Refuge managers put out food during the hardest months of winter.

And *that's* why the Jackson Boy Scouts collect and sell elk antlers every year—to help the great migrating elk herd make it through another severe winter.

Welcome to the National Elk Refuge

The National Elk Refuge was created in 1912 as a result of public interest in survival of the Jackson Hole elk herd. When settlers arrived at the turn of the century, as many as 25,000 elk may have inhabited the valley. Development of the valley threatened the survival of these large herds.

The 24,300-acre National Elk Refuge, administered as part of the National Wildlife Refuge System, U.S. Fish and Wildlife Service, was established to preserve and manage the remaining elk winter range in the valley for the largest concentration of elk in North America. To attain this goal, the refuge maintains extensive grasslands which are managed by irrigation, prescribed burning, and seeding. Stockpiles of alfalfa hay pellets are provided to the elk as supplemental winter food.

Wildlife Watching

While elk are the primary reason for the refuge, it is also a haven for a variety of other mammals and many species of birds. The winter season, between November and May, is the best time to visit and view elk and other wildlife. In spring the elk migrate to the high country and in summer can best be seen at dawn and dusk along roads and trails in Grand Teton and Yellowstone National Parks.

Other wildlife commonly seen on the refuge include mule deer, eagles and coyotes in winter and trumpeter swans, ducks, geese, and sandhill cranes in summer.

Stop by the Refuge Headquarters for bird and mammal lists and other current refuge information.

Current Elk Distribution
Historic Elk Distribution

"When I first moved here, I was really surprised to see so many elk in one spot," said Ken, a Scout in Troop 200. "It was so neat. Now sometimes I think I take them for granted. But if they were gone, it would feel like part of the town was missing."

Dr. Nolan, shown here with his family, was the first supervisor of the National Elk Refuge.

15

The Rocky Mountain Elk Fact Sheet

Family History

Ten million elk used to live in the United States and Canada. But European settlers, who came to America to change their lives, also changed the land around them. By 1900, elk were pushed out of ninety percent of their range. Today there are only about one million elk in North America.

Vital Statistics

Male elk can weigh 500 to 1,000 pounds. Cows weigh in at 400 to 650 pounds.

Birthday

Calves (weighing 30 to 40 pounds) are born in late May or early June.

Life Expectancy

Cows live, on average, twelve years; bulls only seven. The oldest known elk on the Refuge died when it was twenty-nine and a half years old.

The Mating Game

From September through October, bull elk stand guard over groups of cows, trying to keep the females for themselves. Other bulls have the same idea. A bull elk works so hard defending his cows during mating season, he can lose 150 pounds.

Leader of the Pack

Bulls might call the shots during mating season but when it comes to migration older cows run the show. These females lead herds up to a mile long.

Favorite Foods

Elk graze on grass, herbs, and wildflowers. When these aren't available, leaves and branches, even tree bark, will do.

Least Favorite Season

Winter—it takes much more energy to live in cold temperatures and food is harder to find. Still, the elk have some defenses: They grow a thick undercoat of hair for the season. They also try to save body heat by lying down as much as possible. Even so, elk can lose up to one hundred pounds by spring.

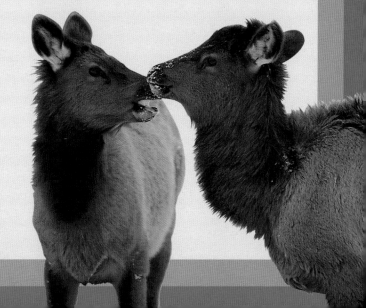

OTHER WILDLIFE ON THE REFUGE

The National Elk Refuge may have been established as a winter haven for elk, but other animals also call it home. The Refuge is filled with meadows and marsh, woods and rocky cliffs, ponds and streams. Each of these areas create the perfect habitat or environment for different kinds of animals.

About fifty species of mammals—from huge buffalo to tiny meadow mice—and 175 species of birds—from our national bird, the bald eagle, to the Canada goose—live on the Refuge. Some of these creatures, like the skunk and mule deer, live on the Refuge all year round. Others, like the pronghorn antelope, move in for a season or two. Still others, like migrating rough-legged hawks, just stop in for a rest and a few meals, on their way from the Arctic to Arizona.

A few hundred bison on the Refuge are reminders of the days when great herds roamed the western plains. When these bison move in to feed, elk get out of their way.

Moose antlers start growing in April. Full sets can weigh up to eighty pounds.

Named for their large ears, mule deer like rugged, hilly countryside.

Coyotes and ravens are the Refuge's clean up patrol. These scavengers quickly eat any elk that die over the winter.

Champions at running and jumping on rocky cliffs, bighorn sheep easily escape predators on steep hills like this one. These sheep's horns keep growing for a lifetime.

Unlike brown pelicans who spot fish from the air and dive into the water, these white pelicans have another way to catch their dinner.

A hundred years ago, when people used their feathers for quills and hats, trumpeter swans were almost hunted to extinction. Now, conservationists are helping these birds make a comeback.

chapter 3

ANTLERS, ANTLERS EVERYWHERE

"Antler avalanche!" Richy called out as he took one antler off the pile,
causing many more to clatter to the floor.

The Pick Up was over but preparation for the auction had just begun. It takes a long time to sort the antlers into sets, bundles, and trailer loads. The Scouts must do this work in a secret place so the valuable antlers aren't stolen.

"Anyone get caught in that last landslide?" Vic Lindeburg laughed as he pulled down another pile. Vic was the Scoutmaster in charge of the auction.

He looked down at the antlers carpeting the floor and grabbed a dark brown one. "I think I've got just the home for this beauty," he said.

Elk are rarely considerate enough to drop both of their antlers at the same time. So, by the time they shed their second antler, they can be miles away from the first. Beautiful racks of antlers, the kind that bring a fortune at the auction, are scattered all over the Refuge.

Fortunately, racks are almost symmetrical, which means the right- and left-handed antlers are almost exact opposites of each other. Unfortunately, to pair them up again, Vic and his helpers had to play the "match game." They first picked

"There are advantages to this job," said Pete, as bone dust flew all over him. "When you go home, your dog loves you."

through their antler piles for the best and biggest. Vic lined up the right-hand antlers on one side. Then he walked down the line with a left-hand antler and looked for its partner. He went from antler to antler, comparing their color, number of points, and the shape of each branch. Once he found a pair, he taped them together.

Of course, the antlers of bull elk that died over the winter from disease or injury were still together—and attached right to their skulls. While Vic was matching separate antlers together, Pete and Jim were sawing apart the antlers from these "winter kills."

"Hey, Pete," said Jim, "why are we taking this guy apart? Are we afraid he's gonna bite somebody?"

Pete explained the new rule that required all skulls be cut. The most valuable hunting trophy, an elk head and antlers mounted on a board, has its antlers attached to the elk's skull. Hunters sometimes poach bull elk just so they can have these trophies. If the Scouts cut the skulls of elk who died during the winter, their antlers become less valuable to trophy lovers buying them at auction. But it lets the Scouts and Refuge send a message: We don't want to encourage or be associated with people who might kill animals illegally.

One way to tell if two antlers are part of the same rack is to compare their first points, or "eye-guards."

21

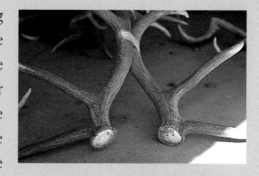

After he finished matching racks, Vic sorted some of the other antlers into bundles. He taped six-pointers with similar shapes together. Then he grouped bunches that had the same dark brown color. Some of the antlers he examined had stories to tell about their former owners. One antler's broken point told of a savage fight for dominance. Another had a bullet hole, proof of that bull's narrow escape from death.

These antlers reminded Vic of a Pick Up just after a great fire had swept through Yellowstone National Park. Someone had found an antler tightly wrapped with forty-five feet of fire hose.

"When that antler dropped," Vic said with a smile, "he was probably the happiest elk on the Refuge."

After all the bundles were taped together, the weighing began. Each bunch was lifted onto a scale then tagged with a number. Meanwhile

After the nicest antlers were bundled for auction, the rest were stacked onto two trailers and sold in two huge lots. Vic pieced them into an antler jigsaw puzzle with little ones in the middle and big ones locking them together.

Vic drove this loaded trailer onto a giant scale. By subtracting the weight of the trailer, the Scouts learned it held 4,060 pounds of antlers, a little over two tons. The smaller trailer held 1,140 pounds.

someone wrote down a description of the bundle so the auctioneer could tell everyone what they were bidding on.

Lot #1: Three antlers, twenty pounds, nice brown color.

Lot #9: A six point by six point matched pair with nice buttons, eighteen pounds.

"This is a monster bundle," said Teri describing Lot #31, six antlers that weighed sixty-one pounds.

Lot #62: Five antlers, perfect for making knife handles, nineteen pounds.

"Sorry, Mr. Bison," said Richy, as he tied a tag through the eye socket of Lot #72, a bison skull taken from the Refuge for auction.

"Let's weigh Gary next and see how much we can get for him," joked B. J.

By the time they tagged the last bundle, everybody was ready for pizza. Stacked in trailers, 7,594 pounds of antler were waiting for auction.

The four huge antler arches in Jackson's town square were built in the early 1960s, before antlers were worth so much.

OTHER USES FOR ANTLERS

Bull elk aren't the only ones who use antlers as a weapon.

Male elk use their antlers as weapons, but people who buy antlers have other ideas. Many antlers go to Asia where they are ground into powder and sold as love potions and medicine. Western artists use others to make earrings and lamps, coat racks, and handles for barbecue forks.

Vic sorted the antlers into bundles with all these different uses in mind. He put antlers with beautiful buttons together because he knew artists carve belt buckles out of this spot where the antler attaches to the elk. Big antlers went into bundles for people making furniture. Dark ones became bundles for people who carve them into knife handles.

Antlers become knife handles, cribbage boards, buttons, and carved belt buckles . . .

. . . or card holders, letter openers, or decorations on baskets.

Even though this belt buckle is made of elk antler, the artist decorated it with a bighorn sheep.

MILLION DOLLAR
PUSH   OPENING AT 12 PM
COWBOY   BAR

In this case, elk antlers become table legs.

The chandelier in this hotel lobby is made of antlers.

The Boy Scouts use about ten pounds of antler each year to make the scarf slides that keep their ties in place.

chapter 4

GOING, GOING, GONE

At 6:00 A.M., on the third Saturday in May, most of Jackson's Scouts were still in bed.
But Vic and a few helpers had already moved the antlers to the town square.

"**H**and me Lot number seventy-five."

"I've got number eighty-six, but where is eighty-seven?"

They worked hard and fast, laying the bundles out in numerical order. Vic and his crew had to display the antlers so buyers could make their choices before the auction began.

Soon a crowd gathered. People had come from all over the country to buy these antlers so they examined them very carefully. They turned over one bundle after another, studying shapes and colors.

One man wanted six antlers to make a chandelier and tried to find two three-piece bundles that looked good together. Another measured matched pairs and imagined them as trophies on his wall. Still another went from bundle to bundle searching for the sturdiest antlers he could find to become legs for his dining room table. They all wrote down the lots they wanted to buy.

Buyers had to register with the auction and receive numbers to use as identification.

B. J. remembered an auction when he carried an enormous set of antlers to a buyer's white car. When B. J. asked what he was going to do with them, the buyer told him to wait a year and find out. "Sure enough," B. J. said, "the next year he came driving up in his huge white Elkmobile. He had mounted that rack of antlers right onto the grill of his car."

At ten o'clock, Vic picked up the microphone at the front of the crowd. "Good morning, everybody. On behalf of the Jackson Boy Scouts, I'd like to welcome you to the Twenty-seventh Annual Elk Antler Auction, the world's only public auction of elk antlers."

A few Scouts let out a cheer as they began to line up. They had started this job by bringing the antlers off the Refuge. They would finish it by carrying them to the auction block, bundle by bundle.

"I hope ours make a lot of money," a Scout murmured as he and his buddy brought the first group up for sale.

"All right, what do we have here?" the auctioneer said as the two Scouts struggled to lift their heavy load high enough for everyone to see.

"Lot number one, three pieces, nice brown color. There are twenty pounds of antler here," the auctioneer

27

After a bundle was sold, the Scouts carried it to its buyer.

"Big Stephe" Stephens (above) has attended every one of the antler auctions. "If you were as ugly as I am," he said posing, "they would take pictures of you too."

said. Then, as if someone flipped his "on" switch, he began talking at a hundred miles an hour.

"I've got seven dollars right here . . . seven, seven, let's hear seven twenty-five, seven twenty-five?"

A man in the crowd nodded. The race was on.

"Seven twenty-five, and fifty? I've got fifty and seventy-five . . . eight, eight, anyone bid eight?"

When the auctioneer named a price, a bidder agreed to pay it with a nod of the head. Then the auctioneer immediately raised the price. Another bidder jumped into the act by waving the number card he'd gotten at the beginning of the sale.

"Now eight's the bid. Will you go eight twenty-five? Now twenty-five. Are you in for eight fifty? And eight seventy-five. I want nine, nine, give me nine . . . thank you, ma'am . . . how about nine and a quarter, nine and a quarter? Anybody in for nine twenty-five?"

Silence. In half a minute, before the Scouts began sweating under the weight of the antlers, the contest was over.

Down went the auctioneer's gavel. "Sold to bidder number twenty-nine for nine dollars. Next is Lot number two, thirty-three pounds of . . ."

"Nine bucks? Hey, for nine bucks let's get a pair of those for the family room," said a tourist who had just walked by.

"For nine bucks, we'd all get a pair for our family rooms and an extra for our bathrooms," said the more experienced woman next to him. "Nine bucks is the price per pound!"

When buyers at this auction bid seven dollars, they are saying they will pay that much for each pound of antler they buy. So that first buyer who pledged nine dollars actually agreed to pay nine dollars multiplied by twenty pounds, or $180 for his antlers. No matter how often the auctioneers explain this rule during the sale, some buyer will think he bid twelve dollars and learn the bill is closer to $312. (Under these circumstances, buyers can change their minds.)

Meanwhile all those weeks of work—gathering, sorting, and tagging antlers—were paying off at lightning speed. One pair of Scouts after another marched their antlers in front of the crowd.

All antlers leaving Wyoming had to be tagged by the state's Game and Fish Department as proof they were acquired legally.

"These antlers are taller than I am," said one of the Scouts who grabbed hold of Lot #59.

"Well, they sure are heavier than I am," grumbled his partner.

"Lot number eighty-five," said the auctioneer, "a pretty set. Don't let 'em get away."

"Hey, you almost poked my eye out," a Scout said as he and his partner made their way to the auction block.

"I got nine seventy-five. I want a ten dollar bill. Make it a ten dollar bill and I'll put this set on wheels."

"I didn't think I was gonna make it," one Cub muttered when he finally put down his bundle.

"We've got a whole crew on this one," the auctioneer said watching three kids struggling with their load. "Lot number one hundred four, we've got thirty-five pounds of antler and one hundred four pounds of boy."

Again and again the gavel hammered out the sale of another bundle.

"Lot number one hundred twenty, sold at twenty-six dollars a pound. The Boy Scouts thank you!"

Finally, the auctioneer announced the last lot, Lot #129. The crowd was quiet as it waited to see how much money the large trailer with over two tons of antlers would bring. After the first pledge for seven dollars, the bidding took off and raced to ten dollars. Then, things slowed down.

"I've got ten, now ten-o-five," the auctioneer said. "Ten-o-five, will you go ten-ten?" Instead of increasing the bid by twenty-five cents like

The Scouts' auction raised $62,205.81 to help feed the elk in their winter refuge.

other times, he started edging the price up by nickels. Doesn't sound like much, but don't forget he was talking about two tons worth of nickels.

"I've got ten-ten, how about ten-fifteen?" he tried again and again. "No?" He slammed down his gavel. "Sold for ten dollars and ten cents!"

A gasp went through the crowd as people did the math in their heads: $10.10 times 4,060 pounds equals $41,006 for the trailer of antlers alone! Things had come a long way since the Refuge gave antlers to visitors as souvenirs in the 1950s, and since the first auction in 1968 when antlers sold for fifty cents a pound.

The total this year: $62,205.81 to help feed the wintering elk!

QUESTIONS OF CONSERVATION

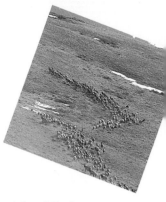

The Scouts work hard to help the elk. But helping wildlife survive in today's world is filled with hard choices.

Most conservationists, people working to save wildlife and wildlife habitat, believe we should let animals live their own lives as much as possible. The things people do, even when trying to help, can have consequences no one ever imagined. In the 1920s, for example, elk on the Refuge were dying. It turned out that the type of hay people fed them cut their mouths and led to fatal infections.

Yet carrying out a philosophy of nonintervention can be painful. Just ask the Scouts who, during one of the antler Pick Ups, found a very sick young calf. It's hard to accept that letting groups of animals live their lives means sometimes letting individual animals die.

Of course, humans control so much of our planet's land, it's impossible not to interfere with wildlife. Again, the elk are a good example. Because we have made parks of Yellowstone and the

Tetons instead of building hotels and golf courses, the elk have plenty of room to live during the summer. But people have taken over so much of the valley, the large number of elk that can survive in the mountains are pressed into too small a space each winter.

Here is another hard choice. Should the size of the elk herd be determined by the number of elk that can live in their summer feeding grounds? That decision means helping out with winter feeding, which weakens the herd by letting some frail elk survive. Or, do we "not interfere" and let the size of the winter feeding grounds determine the size of the herd? That decision means many elk may starve during the cold, hard months.

"I think they should never have started feeding them in the first place" was one Scout's opinion. "But now if they did away with the program, it would do more harm than good."

Since the Refuge does feed the elk, the herd is growing even though there's no more land to give them. Another hard choice: Should they let the number of elk increase and risk the

health of the entire herd? Should they reduce the number of elk by letting some starve? Or, should they reduce the number by letting hunters onto the Refuge? The Refuge gives permits to a certain number of hunters each year to help control the elk population.

What would you do?

33

MISSION ACCOMPLISHED

January in Jackson, the thermometer read twenty-two degrees below zero.
When people's eyes watered, the tears froze on their cheeks.
Fingertips ached within minutes.

Out on the Refuge, the elk bedded down in the snow to save their body heat. That was, until they heard the faintest rumble of the approaching tractor. In a flash, they were up on their feet and on the move.

The feed truck dropped alfalfa pellets, hay pressed into an easier to handle, nutritious form. The pellets made long green lines in the snow and the elk ran up to eat them. Elk, like kids who get more colds in winter because they are shut up together, can catch diseases from each other when they stay in too close a group. So the tractor

In the old days, it took six workers all day to pitch enough hay out of wagons to feed the elk. Now, with alfalfa pellets and trucks, three people do the job in two and a half hours.

released the pellets in thin lines to spread the elk out, and dropped food in four separate areas of the Refuge.

Starting in January, when winter was its cruelest, the Refuge released about seven pounds of pellets a day for each elk. Thirty tons of food a day, every day, until winter melted into spring and the elk followed the retreating snow line back to the high country.

"I'm glad we gather the antlers," said Ken, "because we're using something that comes from the animals to help save them. It's better than making money with a raffle because it's more connected."

Another Scout was just glad they could help, period. "If there weren't any elk," said Josh, "it would take away what the West was."

In a way, the thirty tons of feed a day that the Boy Scouts help provide do keep more than the elk alive. The migration of the Jackson elk is one of the last great journeys of its kind on this continent. So their work helps maintain part of a disappearing past.

"When I first moved here," said Craig, "we would go down to the river early in the morning to watch the elk drink and listen to them bugling. They look so cool."

"Well, I have lived here all my life. So all my life, the elk have been here," responded another Scout. "I can't imagine Jackson without them."

37

GLOSSARY

AUCTION—a sale in which something is sold to the person who offers the highest price

BREEDING SEASON—the time of year when most animals produce their young

BUTTON—the part of the antler that attaches to an elk's skull

CALCIUM—an element that is an essential part of most plants and animals

CARCASS—a dead body

CHANDELIER—a lighting fixture that hangs from the ceiling

CONSERVATIONISTS—people who work to protect the environment

DEFENSES—ways to protect oneself

DOMINANCE—control, influence

EXTINCTION—the state of no longer living or existing

GAVEL—the small hammerlike mallet used by an auctioneer to signal the end of a sale

GENES—the part of a cell that carries inherited characteristics from parent to offspring, for example, skin or eye color in humans

GRAZING—eating grass

HABITAT—all aspects of a plant or animal's home, from its food and shelter to its protection from danger

HAYSTACKS—large piles of hay

HOMESTEAD—a home and its surrounding land

INFECTION—what happens when a germ enters and causes disease in a living thing

MAMMALS—warm-blooded animals with backbones that nourish their babies with milk

MIGRATE—to move from one location to another, in this case, for feeding

MINERALS—natural substances, such as diamonds or quartz, made without any help from plants or animals

NONINTERVENTION—refusal to mix in, stop, or change something

PEDICLES—the bumps on top of an elk's skull from which antlers grow

POACHERS—people who hunt or fish illegally

POINT—each branch of an antler

PREDATORS—animals that live by killing and eating other animals

SAGEBRUSH—a common plant on the western plains of the United States

SCAVENGERS—organisms that live on trash or dead flesh

SNOW LINE—the lower boundary of a snowy area

SPECIES—a group of plants or animals with common qualities

SPIKES—antlers with just one point and no branches

STAMPEDE—the wild run of a group of frightened animals

SYMMETRICAL—having the same shape on both sides of a dividing line

TRESPASS—to go onto land illegally

VELVET—a furry skin covering growing antlers

WAPITI—another word for elk, a Shawnee word meaning "white rump"

WINTER KILLS—animals that die because of the cold winter

FURTHER READING

ABOUT ELK

Arnold, Caroline. *Tule Elk*. Minneapolis: Carolrhoda Books, Inc., 1989.

Patent, Dorothy Hinshaw. *Deer and Elk*. New York: Clarion Books, 1994.

ABOUT THE SCOUTS

Moore, David L. *Dark Sky Dark Land: Stories of the Hmong Boy Scouts of Troop 100*. Eden Prairie, MN: Tessera Publishing, Inc., 1989.

Murphy, Claire Rudolf. *Friendship across Arctic Waters: Alaskan Cub Scouts Visit Their Soviet Neighbors*. New York: Lodestar Books, 1991.

ABOUT KIDS DOING GOOD WORK

Cone, Molly. *Come Back, Salmon*. San Francisco: Sierra Club for Children, 1992.

Hoose, Phillip. *It's Our World, Too: Stories of Young People Who Are Making a Difference*. Boston: Little, Brown, and Company, 1993.

Lewis, Barbara A. *Kids With Courage: True Stories about Young People Making a Difference*. Minneapolis: Free Spirit Publishing, Inc., 1992.